Company General Electric

Instructions for installing and operating bipolar generators

for incandescent lighting

Company General Electric

Instructions for installing and operating bipolar generators for incandescent lighting

ISBN/EAN: 9783337714833

Printed in Europe, USA, Canada, Australia, Japan

Cover: Foto ©ninafisch / pixelio.de

More available books at **www.hansebooks.com**

INSTRUCTIONS

FOR

INSTALLING AND OPERATING

BIPOLAR GENERATORS

FOR

INCANDESCENT LIGHTING

→>◊<←

GENERAL ELECTRIC CO.

SALES OFFICES.

MAIN OFFICES, SCHENECTADY, N. Y.

SALES OFFICES:

BOSTON, MASS., 180 SUMMER STREET.

NEW YORK, N. Y., 44 BROAD STREET.

Syracuse, N. Y., 244 West Fayette Street.

Buffalo, N. Y., Erie County Savings Bank Building.

PHILADELPHIA, PA., 509 ARCH STREET.

Pittsburgh, Pa., 425 Wood Street.

BALTIMORE, MD., 227 EAST GERMAN STREET

ATLANTA, GA., EQUITABLE BUILDING.

CINCINNATI, OHIO, 264 WEST FOURTH STREET.

Cleveland, Ohio, 510 Cuyahoga Building.

CHICAGO, ILL., MONADNOCK BUILDING.

Kansas City, Mo., New York Life Building.

St. Louis, Mo., Wainwright Building.

Dallas, Texas, Corner Field and Main Streets.

DENVER, COLO., 505 16th STREET, KITTREDGE B'D'G.

SAN FRANCISCO, CAL., 15 FIRST STREET.

Helena, Mont., Electric Building.

PORTLAND, ORE., FRONT AND ANKENY STREETS.

Seattle, Washington, Bailey Building.

CANADA, CANADIAN GENERAL ELECTRIC COMPANY, LTD.
TORONTO, ONT.

FOREIGN DEPT. { SCHENECTADY, N. Y.
{ NEW YORK OFFICE, 44 BROAD STREET.

INSTRUCTIONS FOR INSTALLING AND OPERATING EDISON⅃ BIPOLAR GENERATORS.

—

LOCATING AND SETTING OF GENERATORS.

The only proper location for an electric generator is a cool, dry, well ventilated room, free from dust or flying particles of any kind. Basements, unless well drained and well ventilated, should be avoided.

Provide a substantial foundation of timber or mason work and see that it has a suitable footing and is sufficiently heavy and well bonded to check all vibration of the machine.

Take care to guard against irregular settling or distortion of foundation which will throw the armature out of line with the driving shaft. In locating the foundation provide for an easy access to all parts of the generator, and allow for sufficient distance between pulley centers. (See table opposite page 8.)

In constructing the foundation, provision is to be made for the anchor bolts fastening the wooden *base frame.*

The base frame is made of well seasoned timber and should receive several coats of hot asphalt varnish before setting. On this frame the *sliding rails* are placed to allow for moving the generator and adjusting the belt tension. The frontispiece shows the rails and the shifting screw.

The wooden frame serves the very important purpose of insulating the machine from the ground.

Set the generator, if possible, so that the belt pull will come on the under side of the pulley.

B. O. I. 273.

)olt the rails to the base timbers until the armature shaft
ed up with the driving shaft. the belt put on and the
1 for a time. to insure that the alignment is correct.

ie generators are located on a floor above the driving
k device is used instead of the rails for regulating the

ASSEMBLY OF THE GENERATOR.

generators. when marked. should be assembled strictly
the marking

parts of the apparatus clean.   The surfaces of yoke and
must be carefully wiped and cleaned before bolting on
ures. oil or dirt on the joints will reduce the strength of

ature and field coils must be handled carefully, as any
the insulation is likely to cause serious trouble when
·th

ing the armature. use the methods shown on pages 9 and
o allow any weight to come on the commutator. even for

rmature is to be laid on the floor, put a thick pad of
bag of shavings under it.

No 1309 gives the weight. and other data. on armatures.

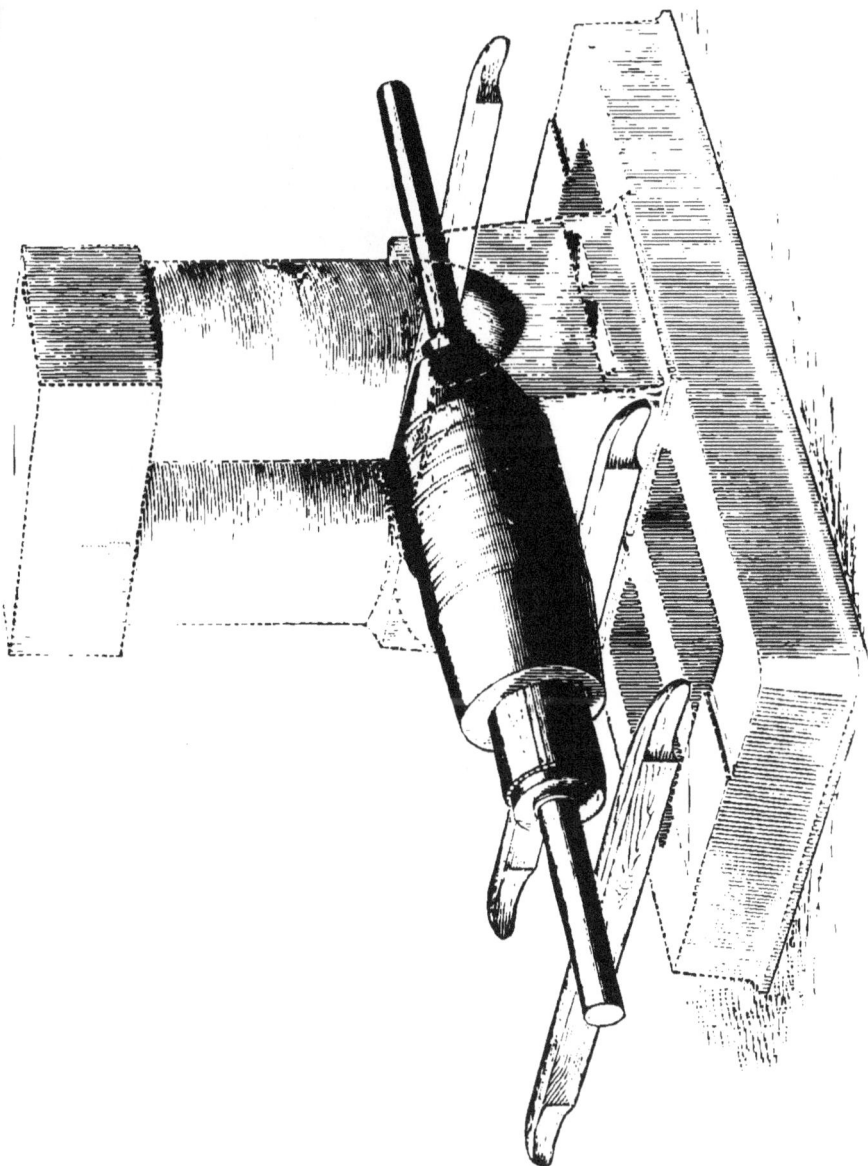

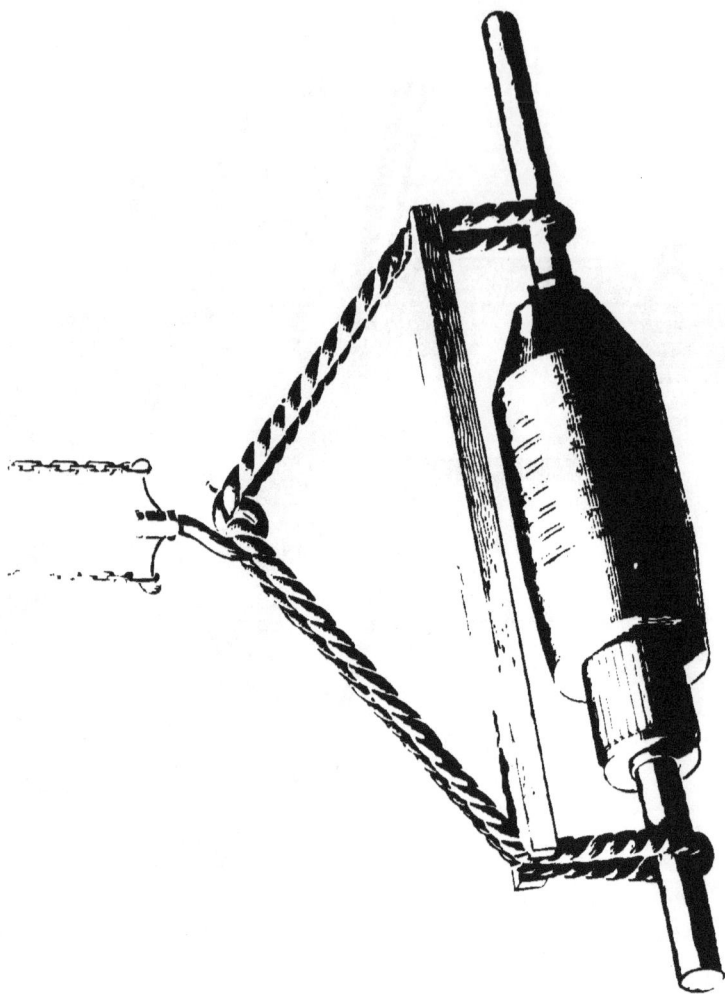

·e must be observed to have the pillow blocks carefully
irfaces clean and well oiled, both on shaft and bearing,
)gether.

important that before a new generator is put at steady
l be first run a few hours at slow speed, which may
ncreased to the maximum. During this trial run
·. carefully attend to the bearings, correct any tendency
liberal supply of oil and scrape the shell if absolutely
the greatest care must be exercised in doing so.*
t all these things are in perfect condition previous to
erator at work on the circuit.

ng a new generator ready to run, having made all the
·ctions (except between it and the bus line), start it up,
·l. and make it generate sufficient current to light its
his will assure you that you actually have it in proper
·roducing a current. Having satisfied yourself on this
·ction can be made to the bus line.

·structions on starting new self-oiling bearings, page 21.

TABLE

Showing Dimensions of Dynamo Base Frames.

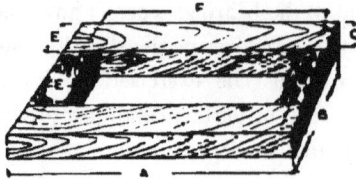

PE OF NAMO.	A.	B.	C.	D.	E.	F.
Kw.	36	36	34		6	19
"	30	30	31		6	19
4 "	34½	36	34		6	35
"	32½	31¾	34		6	34
"	40½	37½	6		9	30
"	47	40	6		6	36
"	46	42	6		9	30
"	50½	46½	6		6	36
"	62	20	6	36	6	60
"	72	54	6	296	11	34
"	82	64	6	34½	12	60
"	91½	75½	6	36½	14	77

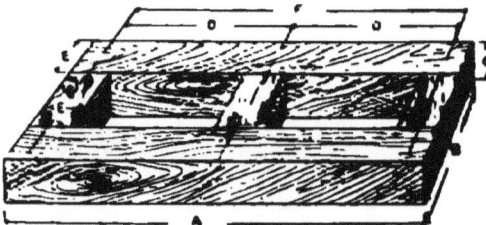

13

CLEANLINESS ABOUT THE GENERATOR IS ESSENTIAL.

All parts of the generator should be kept neat and clean. Dirt, wet dust and oil should not, under any circumstances, be allowed either on any part, especially in crevices near those parts which carrying current.

Copper dust in even small particles may be a source of much annoyance It is very detrimental to the generator, and will seriously injure the durability of the insulation on magnets and armature.

Oil cans, tools, bolts and pieces of iron should be kept away from generator as they are liable to be drawn into the field and injure armature

A good rule is: *Never allow a loose article of any kind to be left upon any portion of a generator.*

They are not only liable to be drawn in, but to fall upon the armature or commutator

Brass or copper oil cans are best to use, as they are non-magnetic.

SWITCHES, CONNECTIONS AND CONTACTS.

A large, clean surface contact is necessary.

The contact surfaces of switches and all connections should be sufficiently firm to secure good conductivity, and be kept clean and bright. All connecting screws should be set firmly and securely in.

When the generator is not in operation leave the switch open. contacts and connections should be frequently inspected, while generator is in operation, to see that there is no undue heating, should be gone over thoroughly at intervals to detect any loose

TABLE

Showing Diameter and Face of Pulleys, Belt Widths, and Minimum Distance between Center of Engine and Generator Pulleys for Edison Standard Generators.

RATING OF GENERATOR IN KILOWATTS.	DIAMETER OF PULLEY IN INCHES.	FACE OF PULLEY IN INCHES.	WIDTH OF BELT IN INCHES.	MIN. DISTANCE BETWEEN CENTER OF PULLEYS IN FEET.
.5	3½	2	1½	6
.75	3½	2½	2	6
1.5	4	3	2	8
3	7½	3	2	10
6	8	4	3	10
8.5	8½	5	4	12
12	9	6	5	12
15	11¼	8	7	12¼
20	12	9	8	13
25	13	10	9	14
30	14	11	10	14
45	17	12	11	15
60	24	13	12	15
100	26	16	15	16
150	44	21	20	16

NOTE. - The above data is based on the assumption that the arc of contact will be fully 180° on each pulley

GENERAL DIMENSIONS OF ARMATURES FOR EDISON BI-POLAR DYNAMOS.

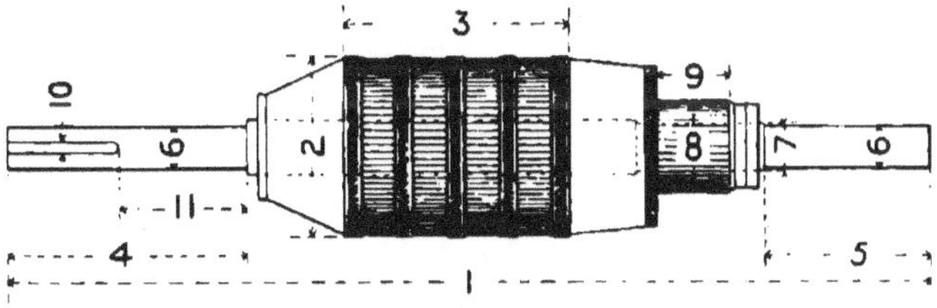

CLASS KW.	NET WEIGHT 125 V.	NET WEIGHT 500 V.	RESIST. 125 V.	RESIST 500 V.	1	2	3	4	5	6	7	8 125 V.	8 500 V.	9 125 V.	9 500 V.	10	11
·5	9	9	3·32		16 3/8	2 15/16	4	4 1/2	2 5/16	1/2	9/16	2		29/32	—	—	—
·75	14 1/2	15	1·66	40	20 13/16	3 1/4	5	5 1/4	2 13/16	5/8	3/4	2 1/4	2 9/16	1 13/16	1 13/16	—	—
1·5	27	27	·815	17	23 7/8	4 5/16	6 1/2	6 1/16	2 7/8	5/8	3/4	2 1/2	2 1/2	2 1/4	2 1/4	—	—
3	60	60	·331	5·8	32 3/16	5 5/16	8	8 11/16	5	7/8	1 1/8	3 3/8	3 3/8	2 1/4	2 1/4	5/16	5 3/8
6	100	100	·116	2·29	37 5/8	6 5/16	9 1/4	10	5 1/2	1 1/8	1 3/8	3 1/2	3 1/2	2 7/8	2 7/8	3/8	5 7/8
8·5	125	125	·068	1·16	42 5/8	6 7/8	10	11 1/4	6 1/4	1 1/4	1 1/2	3 7/8	3 7/8	2 7/8	2 7/8	3/8	6 3/4
12	160	160	·0425	·726	46 7/8	7 1/8	12	13	7 3/4	1 1/2	1 3/4	4 1/2	4 1/2	3	2 13/16	7/16	8
15	220	220	·032	·6	55 1/16	7 3/4	13 1/2	16	9 5/8	1 7/8	2 1/8	4 13/16	4 13/16	4 1/4	4 1/16	1/2	10
20	320	325	·02	·325	63 13/16	8 7/8	15	18	10 3/4	2 1/8	2 3/8	5 1/4	5 3/4	5 1/4	5 1/16	1/2	11 1/2
25	410	410	·0167	·292	66 7/16	9 3/4	16 1/2	19 3/4	11 3/16	2 3/8	2 5/8	5 13/16	6 1/4	5 [illegible]	5 1/16	5/8	12 1/4
30	530	520	·0108	·179	71 13/16	10 5/16	18	22	13	2 3/4	2 15/16	6 5/16	6 1/4	5 3/16	5 1/16	5/8	13 3/4
45	805	800	·009	·162	81 3/4	12 1/4	20 1/2	24	13 5/8	3	3 1/2	6 13/16	8 5/8	5 9/32	5 3/8	3/4	14 1/2
60	1170	1180	·009	·085	90 1/16	13 7/8	24 1/2	27 1/4	14 7/8	3 1/4	3 3/4	6 7/8	7 1/8	5 13/16	5 9/16	3/4	16
100	2155	2105	·00515	·055	102 3/8	17 5/16	25	29 1/2	16 1/8	3 3/4	4 1/2	9 5/16	9 1/4	8 1/8	8 1/2	7/8	19
150 40 V	4880	—	·00252	—	117 5/8	25 1/4	26 1/2	35 1/2	15 5/8	5 1/2	6	12 1/2	—	15 1/8	—	1	21 3/4
150 500 V	—	3700	—	·03	117 5/8	21 11/16	32	35 1/2	15 5/8	5 1/2	6	—	11 7/8	—	9 5/8	1	21 3/4
200 500 V	—	6600	—	·0255	132 1/2	25 1/4	34 1/4	37	21	5 1/2	6 3/8	—	15	—	15	1	22

No. 13038. GENERAL ELECTRIC CO. MAR. 10, '93.

SPEED.

In order to produce the most satisfactory results the generator must be run at its normal speed.

The highest efficiency of the generator is obtained only when running at its proper speed. If the speed falls off, the magnetic field must be made stronger in order to keep the pressure up, and a largely increased amount of current is required to secure a small increase of strength in the magnetic field. The result is that the efficiency diminishes. (See list of speeds, page 16.)

OIL.

The high speed at which the machine runs requires a lubricant especially adapted for such speeds. Uniformity of rotation and absolute reliability are of first importance.

The value of an oil depends more upon its power to reduce friction and prevent the excessive development of heat, than upon its market price. Cheapness can never compensate for inferior quality.

The characteristics which should be possessed by the oil in order to be most efficient as a lubricant for generators are:

1. Sufficient density or body to keep the surfaces, between which it is interposed, from coming in contact under greatest pressure.

2. The greatest adhesion to metallic surfaces, and the least cohesion in its own particles, are qualities of the best oils, and in this respect fine mineral oils stand first.

3. The fluidity of the oil should be as much as is consistent with the above conditions.

Keep the oil free from gritty matter. All foreign matter injures the quality of the oil, and tends to increase the heat of bearings.

New oil should always be filtered.

Economy in the use of oil depends largely upon the method of applying it. By the use of oil cups with adjustable feed a perfectly uniform supply of the minimum safe quantity can be applied to the journal.

Careful experiment will show how many drops of oil per minute required for proper lubrication.

Oil, after passing through the journal, is drawn off from the rior of the pillow block. If of good quality, it has not deteriorated, may be filtered and used over again.

CARE OF OIL CUP BEARINGS.

Attention must be given to the oil cups and bearings of the erator while running. The supply of oil should be constant and 1e minimum amount required for perfect lubrication.

Watch the bearings on a new generator very closely for a few and use oil liberally.

After a machine has been in operation a few days, all bearings d be made to work at a normally low temperature.

Under proper conditions no reasonable excuse can be offered or 11d for abnormal heating. If it exists, it needs immediate stigation and remedy.

After being in operation a short time, a certain amount of heat is rted to the bearings by the armature—any undue heating aside this requires an immediate remedy by the attendant.

The temperature may reach blood heat when running with full

The commutator bearing may be expected to become slightly ner than the pulley bearing.

Undue heating may result from a variety of causes. Among may be mentioned insufficient quantity or poor quality of oil, cr gritty matter in oil, a badly scraped bearing, rough journal, too tight, belt too tight, an armature shaft slightly bent, ings out of line, or generator overloaded.

If from any cause a bearing becomes unduly warm a liberal of oil may be sufficient to check the heat. If it gets very hot screws should be slightly loosened, the oil cup removed, and cooled in water, plentifully applied. It is not advisable, however, water on the interior of the bearing unless sure that it is free dirt or gritty particles.

The cause of the heating should always be ascertained and remedied, and the boxes removed, cleaned, scraped, and accurately refitted before starting up again.

After removing a pillow block be scrupulously careful in replacing to see that the contact surfaces and steady pins are free from grit, fibres of waste, or any kind of dirt.

If the bearings should become considerably worn, there is danger that the armature may rub on the bottom or side of the field blocks, and loosen the binding wires, which is sure to ruin the armature. By observing the position of the armature in the field, it may readily be seen whether the bearings are worn down to any considerable extent.

A small amount of wear downwards may be remedied by raising the pillow blocks with a piece of cardboard or sheet iron. If they are badly worn, or worn sideways, the bearings should be rebabbitted.

BEARINGS OUT OF LINE MAY BE DUE TO:

1. An uneven foundation causing a distortion of generator base;
2. Improper setting and bolting of the pillow blocks;
3. Improper fitting in place of the babbitt shell.

BOXES TOO TIGHT.

This can be remedied by loosening up the nuts holding cap of pillow block; a layer of cardboard of proper thickness may be inserted on the joint under cap and the nuts screwed down.

BELTS TOO TIGHT.

CAUSES.

1. Abnormally short belt.
2. Belt of insufficient width.
3. Belt of poor quality or lacking in thickness.

The pulleys on all generators have been carefully proportioned so that when belts are applied according to specifications, the full load can be pulled without trouble.

BENT ARMATURE SHAFT.

rare occurrence, and can be remedied only by a
iinist.
haft should be straightened very carefully in a lathe.
rue, a pad of cloth or waste and a block rounded to fit
should be used between the end of pry and the
s is an operation requiring care, as the insulation is
m'·d.

OVERLOADED GENERATOR.

cause excessive strain on belt and a necessary
·of; also an abnormal heating of armature, and the
al h·at con/lucted to bearings.

SELF-OILING BEARINGS.

Fig. 3.

A new self oiling bearing for generators has aims to secure absolute reliability against heating as well and economical lubrication

Little attention is required, and there is undue heating than with the ordinary bearing

They can be fitted to existing generators bearings, and are great savers of oil

With the construction shown to set the from the reservoir to both ends of the sleeve which is swept, by the action of the revolving shaft

ie center of the bearing. where it is collected by the central
l returned by the hole to the reservoir, where it has time to
cool By these means a continual circulation of oil through
ig is automatically started. kept up and stopped by the
the shaft. the bearings requiring no attention beyond a
examination and, when necessary, renewal of the oil, which
awn off from the reservoir by a pet cock.

)earing will only act for running in one direction. To run
the other way the sleeve would have to be turned end for
s. therefore. **imperative** that the bearings be correctly put
For this purpose an arrow is stamped on the upper surface
l bearing of the sleeve. and the latter must be set so that
own on the bearing the upper surface of the shaft runs in
on that the arrow points.

earings should be examined once a week. although the oil
equire renewal as often as that.

NOTE.

care and attention must be given to starting a new
with self oiling bearing. or in first use of these new bearings
d generator. Watch them carefully and give frequent
until you are sure that no undue heating will be developed.

CHARGING FIELD MAGNETS.

ie factory the Edison bipolar generators are wound and
n such a manner that the positive (+) current will always be
om the under brush. if the inside end of the R.H. magnet is
l to that brush.

change in the direction of rotation of the armature is
ited for by alteration of the magnet connections on the head
A generator having been once magnetized should always
· retain sufficient residual magnetism to charge itself. If

through accident or otherwise it should become demagnetized, it may be again charged by current from another generator or a gravity or bi-chromate battery may be used.

In charging field magnets with a battery the copper or carbon plate is to be applied to the terminal connected to the under brush. One cell of storage battery, two of bi-chromate or Bunsen, or six of gravity or Le Clanche should be used. The generator current is more satisfactory. To determine the + pole in the case of the generator current, use the ordinary test paper, or put both ends of the wire into a glass of water. Both wires will give off bubbles of gas, but the + much **less** than the —. In testing the generator current a lamp should always be placed in circuit with the testing wires to prevent a short circuit.

In charging the magnets the positive pole of the battery is connected to the terminal of the inside wire of the right-hand coil, facing the head-board, and the negative pole to the left-hand coil. This will make the right-hand pole a south pole, and the left-hand pole a north pole.

In the Central Station generator there are four binding posts for the field lines, two at each end of the switchboard. (See diagram No. 13006.)

The inside terminal of each coil is brought to one or another of these posts according to the direction of rotation.

If the armature revolves from right to left, the terminals of the field magnets must be connected to the inside posts. The left or under brush will then be positive, and the right or upper negative.

If the armature revolves from left to right, the magnet terminals must be connected to the outside posts. The right or under brush will then be positive, and the left or upper brush negative.

The two outside wires of the field magnets should be brought to connecting plates on back board of generator, to which the wires from the regulator are attached.

CONNECTIONS FOR
EDISON BI·POLAR GENERATORS.
CENTRAL STATION.

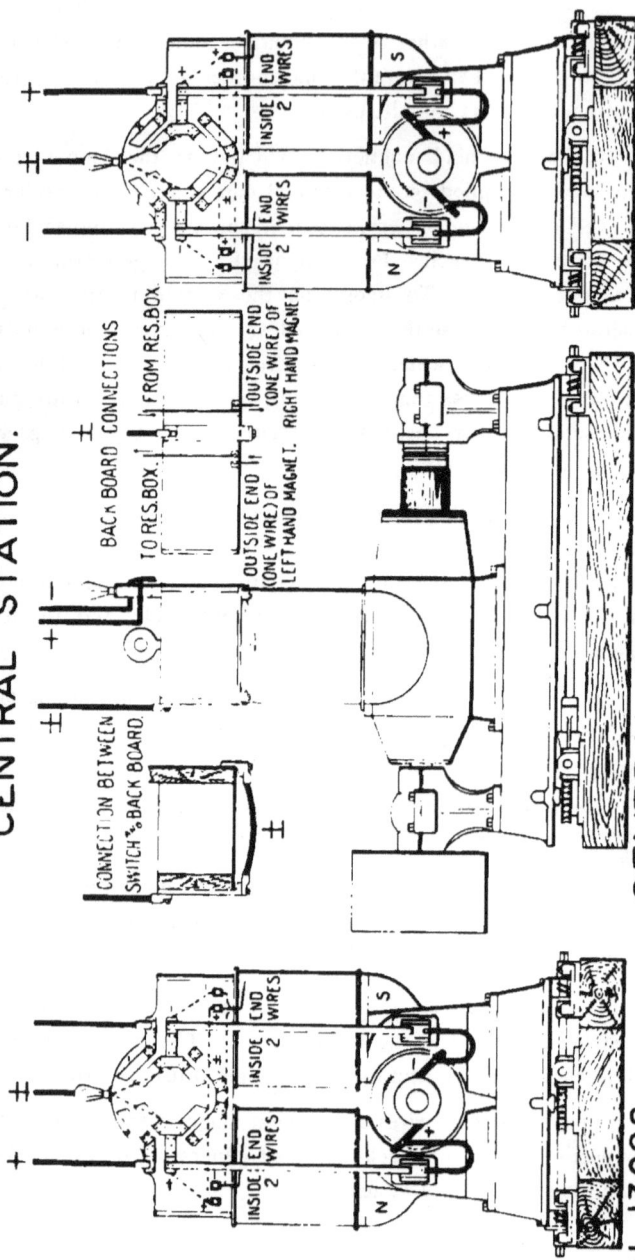

WBC

DEC.17.'92.

GENERAL ELECTRIC CO.

No.13006.

+

±

−

±

+

INSIDE END
WIRES

2 INSIDE
END WIRES

S

N

+

INSIDE END
2 WIRES

INSIDE END
WIRES

S

N

+

±

+

±

BACK BOARD CONNECTIONS

TO RES.BOX.

FROM RES.BOX.

OUTSIDE END
(ONE WIRE) OF
LEFT HAND MAGNET.

OUTSIDE END
(ONE WIRE) OF
RIGHT HAND MAGNET.

CONNECTION BETWEEN
SWITCH & BACK BOARD.

±

±

+

In both cases, when the magnets are charged, so that the right-hand pole is the south pole, and the left-hand the north pole, the under brush is positive.

The polarity of the coils should never be reversed.

If by any chance the polarity of the field magnets becomes reversed, the field connections remaining as above, the conditions described will be reversed.

The polarity of the wires is reversed either by reversing the polarity of the field magnets or the direction of rotation of the armature.

Reversing the polarity of a generator does not impair its efficiency

TESTING FIELD AND ARMATURE.

The generator must at intervals be disconnected from the circuit and throughly tested to make sure that the armature and field wires are free from leakage between the windings and the base. This test should be made at regular intervals with a Galvanometer and Rheostat, and a record kept of the readings.

If a galvanometer is not to be had, use a magneto bell.

The insulation between the body of the generator and all parts of the circuit must be perfectly maintained. Avoid loose coils or loops in the field connections. If the insulation on the flexible cables leading from brushes becomes worn after long use have it renewed.

A standard insulation of one megohm should be maintained from armature and fields to base and from base to earth.

The faults which are liable to occur in both field magnets and structure coils are as follows:

A cross between separate coils, or turns of a coil which are side by side, or cross each other.

When this occurs in magnets a portion of the coil is cut out, and its strength is diminished. A fault of this kind in the armature results in a loss of power, and possibly in burning out of the faulty coils.

A generator may still work with a large part of its field coils short
ited. Such a condition is shown by one magnet coil getting
·r than its mate, accompanied by sparking at the brushes.

Each coil of armature and each side of field magnet should be
rately tested.

If a magnet coil is grounded at two points the current is shunted
nd a portion of the coil, as in the first case.

If two armature coils of considerable difference of potential are
nded on the core, they will probably be burned out, and in any
t will reduce the power of the generator.

In either case the fault may be detected by testing the insulation
e coil. Each coil of armature must be tested separately.

The insulation resistance of the whole armature to ground may
·st given.

In stations operated less than twenty-four hours per day, a careful
should be made for crosses or grounds before steam is turned on.

This test should be made sufficiently early to insure the correction
·· trouble (should any be found) before the hour of starting the
·n.

In starting, the generators connected with the system should be
without pressure and gradually raised to proper E. M. F.; this
develop any fault originating since making test, and before any
ge is done to either the system or apparatus.

The positive and negative sides of the system should be
intently indicated on all the conductors and electrical apparatus
· station.

A good plan to follow is for positive, use letter ".A" in red;
tive, use letter " B " in blue.

The electrical apparatus of the station should be so arranged
a circuit switch is provided for each generator.

This circuit switch should be used for throwing the generator in
out of circuit.

On C. S. generators a changing switch is mounted on the machine, and should not only be used for changing the generator over from one side of a three-wire system to the other, but should be used for throwing the generator in and out of circuit.

Each side of the switch should be prominently lettered to indicate respectively the "A" and "B" sides of the system.

OPERATING A PAIR OF GENERATORS IN SERIES.

Before starting up a pair of generators, inspect thoroughly every part, and have brushes, switches and connections in perfect order.

The engine should be gradually warmed and started a short time before the generators are needed, and kept turning slowly. They are then in readiness for instant use when needed.

If this precaution is omitted, trouble is likely to result in the hurry and confusion of a sudden demand for light.

The following order of procedure should be observed for starting up:

1. Fill oil cup and adjust feed. (If old style bearings are used.)

2. Get full speed on engine and armatures of both generators. Be sure that all switches are open, belts properly tightened, and everything in perfect order.

3. Adjust the brushes to both commutators. They should be in No. 3 position as shown on page 33.

4. Make sure that the fields of both generators are charged up properly. The strong attraction of a piece of iron will indicate that the field is made.

If a generator is thrown in multiple with other generators before its field is charged, a short circuit will be formed through its armature, and it may be burnt out.

5. Throw in generator galvanometer on first generator, and regulate pressure to the proper electro motive force.

One side of the generator galvanometer is connected to the neutral "Bus." The other side is connected to a switch, from which

29

UNEQUAL DIVISION OF LOAD.

In the case of a pair of generators in series on the three-wire system, the division of load will depend on the balancing of the lights on the system, as well as on the pressure between the two sides. If pressures are all right an unequal division would indicate an unbalanced condition of the system which should be at once corrected.

If a generator is in multiple with another it may, if its pressure is too high, assume a portion of the load of the second generator, or even drive it as a motor. Overloading of the generator and heating of the armature is the result.

The obvious remedy is to regulate the pressure at once from the resistance boxes, by throwing resistance in the field of the first and throwing it out of the field of the second. This must be done very gradually.

When throwing a generator out observe the pressures on the system, and adjust the regulators of the remaining generators to keep the pressure at the proper point, also adjust all brushes to the increased load. The loads on both generators should be worked down together, and the second generator cut out as soon as possible after the first.

Generators should never be switched out on full load, except in case of extreme emergency.

The brushes should not be raised until the lamp on the headboard ceases to show incandescence. If this point is neglected the discharge of the field magnet coils may break the lamp, jump to base of machine or cause other trouble.

Having thrown out both generators, raise the brushes and clean and polish the commutators (if necessary) before stopping the engine in order to have them in readiness for the next run.

Shut down the engines slowly, and stop the oil feed.

The generators should then be thoroughly cleaned of oil, dirt and copper dust, and put in perfect order for the next run.

The engine should never be slowed down before the circuit hes are thrown out. Failure to observe this rule may result in ing out armatures.

Make sure that the open switches and lifted brushes are securely in position against any chance of getting loose and unintention- closing the circuit. which might result in serious damage.

IN SHUTTING DOWN FINAL PAIR OF GENERATORS.

In shutting down a system when only one pair of machines are ing. shut down the engine and do not touch the resistance box. is method be used there will be practically no sparking or stment of brushes required. Operate switches. and lift the ies

COMMUTATOR.

Special care and attention must be given to the commutator.

The perfect or imperfect condition of the commutator in a al station is strong evidence of the competency or incompetency he attendants. There is a certain knack in caring for a mutator easily acquired by any careful and painstaking man.

Prevention, not cure. is the correct rule for commutator troubles. life of a well cared for commutator should not be less than two al continuous running. and maybe more. A little roughness is removed but if allowed to increase it will soon be too late for cure by except the lathe.

The commutator should at all times present a clean and polished and a true circumference. It is in its best condition when has a dark glazed surface. free from scratches. If accidentally cld it may be polished with No. oo sand paper moistened with of sperm oil or vaseline. and cleaned with a piece of canvas or chois skin. Emery paper or emery cloth should not be used to scour the commutator, as the fine particles of emery, settling in the divisions between the bars, will cause short circuiting at the commutator. A file should not be employed except for specia purposes.

Waste should not be used to clean the commutator, as the lint i apt to get under the brushes and cause sparking.

Avoid the use of all special kinds of grease or wax offered fo sale for use on commutators; they do much more evil than good, and should not be permitted in the station.

If the commutator is but slightly rough or uneven or out of true it may be ground down by the use of sand paper in a block hollowed out to fit its true circumference. If in very bad condition, however it should be turned down with a tool and special rest made for the purpose.

For turning off commutators a slide rest can be obtained from th Schenectady Works and is made to attach to the generator bed This will save removing the armature, provided a proper slow speed can be had. If an armature has to be removed for any cause th greatest pains must be taken in handling. Armatures are ofter burned out because of some blow or bruise received from careles handling.

Do not lay an armature on the floor unless some sort of cushion i placed underneath. Armatures should be lifted and carried by th shaft as far as possible.

In turning off commutator the cut should stop before reaching the end of the bar. This is important to preserve the insulation and to keep the iron collars intact for receiving a new set of bars.

The amount of wear on commutator which may be allowed befor sending to shops for repairs depends on the depth of the commutato bars, and the amount of current they are required to carry. Thi varies in different machines.

The safe depth to which the commutator may be worn in eac machine should be known, and a new commutator supplied before th dangerous point is reached.

The following table shows the original diameters of commutators and the diameters to which they may be safely worn for different sizes of generators:

COMMUTATORS FOR EDISON BIPOLAR DYNAMOS.

'85 TYPE, 125 VOLTS.

KILOWATTS	NUMBER OF BARS	LENGTH OVER ALL	LENGTH OF BRUSH SURFACE	DIAM. OF BORE OF SHAFT	OUTSIDE DIAM. OF COMMUTATOR	ALLOWED FOR TURNING DOWN	LEAST SAFE DIAM. OF COMMUTATOR
.5	32	2	1		2		1⅞
.75	42	3½	1⅞	⅞	2¼		1⅞
1.5	52	4	2¼	⅞	2¼		1⅞
3	44	4½	2¼	1½	3⅞		2½
6	56	5	2⅝	1⅞	3¼		2
8.5	48	5½	2⅞	1¼	3⅞		2⅛
12	50	5¼	3	1⅞	4¼		3⅞
15	48	7	4⅞	2¼	4⅞		3⅞
20	62	8	5¼	2¼	5¼		4
25	62	8	5	2¼	5⅞		4½
30	56	8½	5¼	2½	6⅞	1½	4⅛
45	52	9½	5⅞	3½	6⅞	1¼	5⅞
60	40	9½	6⅞	3½	6¼	1½	5¼
100 140 volts	48	13½	8	4½	9⅞	1½	6¼
150 140 volts	41	21	15⅞	6	12¼	1⅞	9⅞

It is assumed that the diameter is kept the same for the whole length of the commutator, and that the section of the bars at the dangerous point is just equal to the section of the wire of the armature.

It sometimes happens that a bar in the commutator will spring up and stand a little higher than the rest. This will cause the brush to vibrate and occasion sparking on account of imperfect contact. The generator should be stopped as soon as possible, and the high bar carefully filed down to a true circumference.

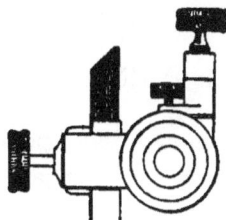

Position of Brushes,
1 Full Load
2 Light Load
3 No Load

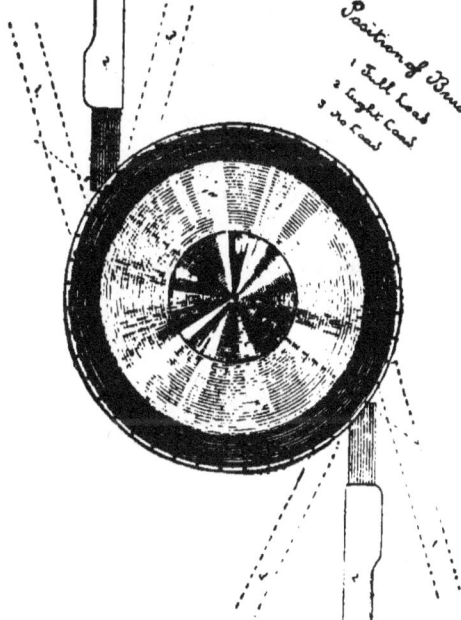

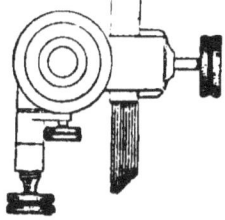

THE NEUTRAL POINT.

The neutral points of a generator are those positions on the commutator between which the difference of potential is the greatest and where there is the least difference of potential between adjacent bars. These points are diametrically opposite.

The position where there is no sparking of the brushes, or the non-sparking point, does not exactly coincide with the neutral point when there is a load on the machine. The non-sparking point advances faster than the point of highest electro-motive force, and they are further apart the greater the load.

The neutral point changes with the change of load. With a slight load the neutral point is near the extremities of a horizontal diameter. As the load increases the neutral point moves forward in the direction of rotation, and the brushes must be advanced to the non sparking point.

ADJUSTMENT OF BRUSHES.

In order to maintain the commutator in proper condition and reduce the wear to a minimum, it is vitally necessary that a proper adjustment of the brushes be secured. They should work absolutely free from sparks. Any sparking whatever indicates a bad condition of the commutator or defective adjustment of the brushes.

Woven wire brushes can be used in the standard brush-holder by removing the trough and stiffening the brush with strips of hard copper called "brush guides."

The brushes should be firmly fastened in the holders in order to insure good conductivity and avoid heating, and placed at the proper angle to secure the best contact surface.

The end of the brush should be carefully beveled so as to conform accurately with the surface of the commutator. The brush should bear lightly upon the commutator, and every part of the

beveled end should rest upon it. The pressure should b
sufficient to insure good contact and avoid all cutting and scra₁

One of the worst causes of sparking is lack of pressure
brush on the commutator, caused by improper setting of the
holder stud or by allowing a brush to wear too short. The
angle of the end of the brush is about 45 degrees. To mainta
as the brush wears it must be pushed forward in the holder froₗ
to time. If this is not attended to, the brush holder will be held
the stop pin. pressure is relieved and imperfect contact or nonₗ
is the result.

When at rest the brushes should always be raised fro
commutator. and held away by the clips provided for the purpoₗ

If left in contact with the commutator they are liable
injured or perhaps ruined by an accidental reversing of the diₗ
of rotation.

The ends of the brushes, where they rest upon the comm
should not be allowed to become dirty. rough or ragged, nor
the strands be allowed to spread.

The brushes should at frequent intervals be removed.
trimmed, ends filed and reset.

They may be cleaned from oil by washing in benzine.

Bipolar generators can be operated under full load with absₗ
no spark at the brushes.

It is very necessary that persons in charge of generatorₗ
appreciate this fact. and always aim to secure this condit
operation.

A generator in operation with a spark at brushes is *primₗ*
evidence of carelessness or ignorance on the part of the atte
and no central station manager should tolerate such a condit
affairs or accept any excuse whatever for its continuance.

COPPER WOVEN WIRE BRUSHES.

EDISON BIPOLAR.

Length.	Width.	Thickness.	Angle of Bevel.	On Each Stud.	Per Machine.	Brushes.	Brush Filing Jig
3	1¼	5½	45°	1	2	57111	57206
4½	2	⅞	45°	2	4	57112	57207
4½	2	⅞	45°	2	4	57112	57207
7	8¼	½	45°	2	4	57113	57208
7	1⅜	5½	45°	2	4	57114	57209
7	1⅝	½	45°	2	4	57114	57209
7	1⅞	½	45°	2	4	57114	57209
0	1¼	1½	45°	2	4	57115	57210
0	1½	1½	45°	2	4	57115	57210
0	1¾	1½	45°	2	4	57115	57210
0	1¼	1⅜	45°	2	4	57115	57210
0	1⅝	½½	45°	2	4	57115	57210
0	1½	1½	45°	3	6	57116	57211
2	1¾	⅜	45°	3	6	57117	57212
-	1¼	⅞	45°	6	12	57117	57212
2	1¼	⅞	45	6	12	57117	57212

COPPER WIRE BRUSHES.

Kw.	.5	.75	1.5	3	6	8.5	12	15	20	25	30	45	60 125v	60 500v	100 140v	100 500v	150 140v
Number of Brushes. On each Stud.	1	2	2	2	2	2	2	2	2	2	2	2	3	3	3	3	6
Number of Brushes. Per Machine.	2	4	4	4	4	4	4	4	4	4	4	4	6	6	6	6	12
Number of Prongs.	1	1	1	1	2	2	2	3	3	3	3	3	2	2	3	3	3
No. of Layers Beveled. 125v.	2	4½	4½	4½	4½	4½	4½	6	6	6	6	6	9	5	9	6	9
No. of Layers Beveled. 500v.								4½	4½	4½	6	6					
Thickness.		8¾	8¾	3½	3½	3½	5½	3½	4½	3½	3½	3½	3½	5½	8	4½	4
Width.	7/16	2	2¾	8¼	1 1/8	1 1/8	1 8	1 1/8	1 1/8	1 1/2	1 1/8	1 1/8	1 1/8	1 1/8	1 1/8	1 1/8	1 1/8
Length.	3	4½	4½	6	6	6	6	8	8	8	8	8	9	9	12	8	12
Brush Filling Jig Catalogue No.				57300	57300	57300	57300	57303	57303	57303	57303	57303	57301	57302	57304	57303	57304

Before starting up, the brushes must be adjusted so that their ends rest on the commutator at diametrically opposite points. Opposite bars of the commutator can be found by counting them.

Table Giving Number of Sections in Commutators of Different Sizes of Generators.

kw	3	6	8.5	12	15	20	25	30	45	60	100	150
Sections.	44	58	48	50	42	66	66	58	52	50	48	41

As a result of the brushes not being diametrically opposite, it will be impossible to get them both exactly on the neutral point, and a spark will be produced.

Sparking at the brushes results from a variety of causes.

Sparking is expensive and detrimental chiefly because it results in burning the brushes and commutator, hastening their frequent renewal. Every spark consumes a particle of copper, torn from the commutator or brush. The longer the sparking continues the greater the evil becomes, and the remedy must be applied without delay.

SPARKING, CAUSES AND REMEDIES.

1st C. Brushes not set at neutral point.

R. The brushes having been previously set diametrically opposite, they can be readily adjusted to the neutral point by moving the rocker arm backward or forward until the non-sparking point is found.

2d C. Brushes not set at diametrically opposite points.

R. Great care must be taken to have the brushes set diametrically opposite before starting, as their readjustment while running is troublesome. If any individual brush sparks while the other brushes are working perfectly, it is out of alignment.

To adjust, shift brush in holder until non-sparking point is

3d C. Brushes set so as not to get full bevel to the circumference of commutator.

R. If brushes are set crooked, and do not bear evenly on the commutator, sparking is apt to result. Readjustment must be made to secure full face of brush at proper bevel.

4th C. Brushes set with insufficient pressure.

R. This fault can often be remedied by increasing tension on spring in brush holder.

If all brushes on same side have too little pressure, loosen large nut on end of brush-holder bar and turn bar slightly toward commutator, tighten nut firmly and give careful attention to adjustment of spring. This can be done when generator is stopped.

5th C. Brushes spread apart and filled with dirt and oil.

R. Oil and copper dust and dirt will fill in between the wires and spread the brushes. All this can be removed by a thorough washing in benzine or a hot solution of sal-soda water, or strong potash water. With proper care this will not require to be done oftener than once a week.

6th C. Brush having loose or crooked wire on edge.

R. Loose or crooked wires on edge of brushes are usually caused by careless management in putting brush in holder.

If this trouble occurs accidently while in operation, carefully bend the loose wire back and clip it off close to the body of the brush.

Any loose wire causing sparking should be removed.

7th C. Brush with hard burnt ends, which destroy its pliability and increase the resistance at contact with the commutator.

R. Brushes, if so badly burned that pliability is lost, must be thrown away; but, if still pliable and of sufficient length, cut off the burnt portion and file to proper bevel in the brush filing jig.

8th C. Commutator bars loose, high or low.

R. A single high bar in the commutator will vibrate the brush, causing poor contact, and consequent sparking. A heavier tension must be applied to the spring of the brushes until the run is over. As soon as possible the generator should be stopped and the high bar carefully repaired.

If commutator bars are loose, screw up the ring at end of commutator.

If bar is high. set it down in place with a wooden mallet and screw up the ring.

If bar is low. screw the ring up firmly in·place and turn the commutator down to a true circumference, or grind it down with sand paper in a hollow block.

9th C. Loose connection between armature coil and commutator bar.

R. A loose or broken connection between commutator and armature coil will cause a peculiar blue snapping spark, just as the bar leading to it is passing under the brush.

This will show itself on the particular bar having the loose connection.

This spark cannot be wholly remedied while running. The spark may be diminished by setting one brush on each side a little in advance of the other. The generator should be stopped as soon as possible and the connection of the armature carefully examined and any loose joints properly repaired.

Take off covering over connections. loosen screws holding connections together.

See to it that the soldering on joint is thoroughly sweated in. and the little pocket holding ends of wire is filled with clean solder making a perfect joint.

Clean all surfaces. tighten up screws firmly. and renew canvas covering over end of armature.

Be sure that this covering is always strong and whole. do not permit it to get ragged and let in copper dust.

10th C. Section short circuited. either in commutator or armature coils

R. This fault cannot be repaired in station unless there is an expert man on hand who knows how to wind an armature. The armature will probably require to be sent to district office for repairs.

11th C. Armature damp, with consequent short circuiting of coils.

R. A damp armature can generally be dried out by setting it near a stove or steam radiator, where it will be exposed to moderate heat.

12th C. Short circuit or cross on outside system.

R. A cross will cause brushes to spark and sputter severely. The cross must be burnt out promptly.

13th C. Commutator dirty, oily, rough, worn in ridges, or out of true circumference.

R. Oil and dirt can be wiped off with a piece of canvas or chamois; then polish commutator with fine sand paper. Ridges should be scoured down with sand paper. A commutator out of true should be turned down with a tool and slide rest, using a slow speed and a fine cut (see special instructions, page 30).

14th C. Generator overloaded.

R. This cause of sparking is easily detected at the ampere meter. The proper measures should be taken at once to relieve the machine. If the load on a pair is unequally divided it should be properly regulated by means of the resistance boxes. It due to a heavy load of lamps, or short circuit on the line, the overloaded generator can be relieved by throwing an additional generator in multiple and with it.

As an ampere meter is not infallible it is well to notice the temperature of the armature, if a generator is doing heavy duty.

The test of temperature can be made by laying a glass thermometer close against the armature immediately on stopping the generator.

the lamps connected on the system are so great in number as
se an overload of all the generators every night, then an
nal pair of generators should be ordered at once.

h C. Armature coils or commutator sections short circuited
imulations of copper dust.

R. An examination of some generators would lead a man to
the machine was constructed for the purpose of producing
dust.

e accumulation of copper dust on a generator and its gradual
tion into the coils of armature and fields, is often the real
f serious accident and expensive repairs.

is is one of the principal features which denotes carelessness
fficient management, and an utter lack of appreciation of the
ince of cleanliness about generators and electrical apparatus.

e remedy is easy to apply; the generators MUST be kept clean
nd copper dust.

ould the operator not be perfectly familiar with the work
d in any of the remedies suggested in the foregoing, he should
lertake it, but return the apparatus to the nearest repair shop
General Electric Company, where proper facilities are at hand
ng such work.

FAULTS AND ACCIDENTS.

s only in times of accident that we develop in a central station
tendent some of the most necessary qualifications for this
r that his inability is made manifest. Presence of mind, calm
ut, quick action — all combined — enabling him to do just the
hing in an emergency on the spur of the moment, are all
int.

ien accidents happen in an electric light station they come
and no time is to be lost in applying the proper remedy.

perience and perfection of system have enabled us largely to
roubles which in early days were of frequent occurrence.

The faults and accidents to which generators are liable are very rare, and may be largely avoided by careful inspection and proper care. When accidents occur, the cause must be quickly perceived and the remedy intelligently applied.

The following are some of the disorders:

BURNING OUT ARMATURE COIL.

This may be occasioned by overloading the armature, causing the insulation of the coils to give way, and is indicated by the armature suddenly beginning to smoke. The coil is thus rendered useless. As a temporary makeshift, the injured coil may be disconnected from the commutator, the ends insulated with tape, and the two adjacent bars to which the coil was connected, joined to each other by a wire not smaller than the armature wire.

The machine can be operated for a time in this way, but a new armature should be put in as soon as possible.

RING OF FIRE AROUND THE COMMUTATOR.

This is caused by small particles of copper betweeen the bars of the commutator, making a local short circuit from bar to bar across the mica insulation.

To remedy it, clean the commutator carefully, and do not allow the brushes to cut and scratch it.

BREAKING DOWN OF ONE GENERATOR.

If one generator of a single pair operating on a three wire system breaks down from any cause, the break down switch should at once be thrown, providing the total number of lamps burning does not exceed the capacity of the remaining generator, which will then be supplying current for those lamps on, practically, a two-wire system. Should the total number of lamps burning exceed the

capacity of the remaining generator, those on the side of the disabled
generator must be thrown off, the remaining generator simply
supplying current to its own lamps. In this event, the break-down
switch will not be used.

*In any case the disabled generator should be thrown off the system
at once.*

REVERSAL OF POLARITY OF MAGNETS.

Reversal of polarity of a generator which is one of two or more
connected in multiple is equivalent to a dead short circuit, and, if it
does not blow a fuse or throw off a belt, will probably burn out an
armature.

Reversal of polarity of one of a single pair of generators working
in series on a three-wire system will tend to send all the current
through the neutral wire, which will cause the lights to burn dim, and
charge up the current to the company on all meters on the reversed
side.

If the reversed generator should be switched in with another not
reversed on the same side further trouble is caused. If generators
supplying current through meters should all be reversed, the meters
will all be caused to read backward.

Each man having a generator under his care, should be perfectly
familiar with the proper methods of charging a reversed or demagnetized field.

A compass for testing polarity can be had for a small sum. In
an emergency a magnetized steel needle attached to a silk thread will
answer every purpose. Do not trust to the mark on the compass, but
see for yourself which way it points, and remember that the north
pole of the compass points to the south pole of the generator.

Generators on the three-wire system may be reversed under the
following conditions:

A reversal of the polarity of the field magnets sometimes takes
place when starting up.

This may be due to the influence of another generator in close proximity to it.

The induction of a strong magnet may be sufficient to reverse the slight permanent magnetism of the generator at rest.

THE FIELD OF A GENERATOR MAY BE REVERSED:

By the current of a second generator in series with it while in operation, if the brushes of the first generator are accidentally raised or its current broken in any way between the points to which the field circuit is connected.

By lifting the brushes before throwing out the switch.

By burning out the safety catches which are on some of the old style generators.

By crosses on the lines.

By 200 volt motors. This is more apt to occur during a light load, when the motor is thrown on with a heavy load.

If one side of the system becomes reversed, it will show the fact by low pressure and by the indicators on that side reversing, and by the neutral "bus" becoming very hot and the neutral ampere meter indicating a very heavy load; also, no difference of potential between + and — "bus."

To correct the machines open the circuit switch, raise the brushes and throw the generator-changing switch on the side not reversed, and leave it about a minute. Then, after raising the field on it, test the polarity of the machine with test paper, or by the methods mentioned on page 44.

EFFECTS OF LIGHTNING.

Lightning is to be feared as a property-destroying agent merely. One of the safest places to be in during a thunder storm is an electric light station. Where damage has happened to a generator caused by lightning, the occasion has been found in the absence of the proper safeguards or in some faulty work in connection with them.

No effects of lightning will be felt on Edison systems with street conductors entirely underground. Where there are very long outdoor pole lines similar effects occur as on telegraph and telephone lines, and somewhat similar precautions should be taken to prevent injury to apparatus.

The usual result of lightning freaks are the breaking of lamp carbons, melting of fuses, and damaging of generators, by injury to the insulation or reversing and demagnetizing.

For the protection of the generator in systems having long overhead lines special precautions should be taken in the way of perfectly insulating the base from the ground. Direct connection of water or drip pipes to the generator is to be avoided, and even the proximity of such pipes, when lightning is specially to be guarded against, is objected to. Lightning arresters, when used, should be in plain sight. Fuses on such arresters must be promptly replaced. Ground wires and connections are particularly important and must be kept intact and in good condition.

The following will always guide you in recharging a generator:

I.—Raise the brushes of the demagnetized or reversed generator.

II.—By the double changing switch throw it in multiple arc with one which is running all right on the other side of the system.

III.—Close the single generator switch for an instant.

This does not take over thirty seconds.

The previous instructions given for tests of field and armatures for crosses and grounds, and also for demagnetization and reversal of polarity fully cover the important points for immediate investigation of damage and the proper remedy to apply.

CROSSES ON STREET CONDUCTORS.

These troubles are not of frequent occurrence and principally happen on overhead systems, due to severe storms causing the dropping of telephone or telegraph wires across the electric light circuits

It is estimated that all crosses can be prevented by the use of wire having durable weather proof insulation, and by careful and thorough construction of the pole line system. Nevertheless, the fact remains (in the absence of these precautions, in many cases due to lack of original investment) that crosses occur, and it therefore becomes our duty to give such instructions as will enable the station operator to clear his lines and thus avoid more serious damage.

In this particular the operators must work with promptness and decision.

When a leak appears on the system, whether a ground or a cross, additional generators must be thrown in on the faulty side. As much current as possible must be forced into the leak, in order to burn out the fault or safety fuses, if possible, and to keep the lights up to candle power.

The fault should then be located and corrected at once.

If a heavy cross or ground shows on the line, and the lights burn low or go out, vigorous measures must be taken at once. Such a fault usually occurs when there is a light load on the system, and insufficient current being generated to melt the safety fuses.

To clear out the cross, start up two or three generators, and get their pressures up until the pilot lamps show somewhat less than full candle power.

The changing switches should be so adjusted as to throw all the generators on the faulty side.

Then everything being in readiness, at a given signal close all the circuit switches. At the same instant the rocker arms should be pulled over and the brushes adjusted. To achieve success, the men must act in unison and quickly.

If the fault is not cleared, the generators must be thrown out and the operation repeated with more generators.

The above described method is usually successful in clearing the fault or fusing the nearest safety catches, after which the lights on that side will come up again.

CAUTION.

Great care must be taken, when the fault disappears, that the pressure on the system does not come up too high and injure the lamps

FACTS TO BE REMEMBERED.

1. Be sure that the speed of the generator is right.
2. Be sure that all the belts are sufficiently tight.
3. Be sure that all connections are firm and make good contact.
4. Keep every part of the machine and generator room scrupulously clean.
5. Keep all the insulations free from metal dust or gritty substances.
6. Do not allow the insulation of the circuit to become impaired in any way.
7. Keep all bearings of the machine well oiled.
8. Keep the brushes properly set and see to it that they do not cut or scratch the commutator.
9. If the brushes spark, locate the trouble and rectify it at once, AS NO EXCUSE WILL BE ACCEPTED FOR SPARKING.
10. The durability of the commutator and brushes depends on the care exercised by the person in charge of the generator.
11. At intervals the generators must be disconnected from the circuit and thoroughly tested for leakage and grounds.
12. In stations running less than 24 hours per day, the circuit should be thoroughly tested and grounds removed (if any are found) before current is turned on.
13. Before throwing generators in circuit with others running in multiple, be sure the pressure is the same as that of the circuit, then close the switch.
14. Be sure each generator in circuit is so regulated as to have its full share of load, and keep it so by use of resistance box.

Each central station manager is advised to drill his subordinates (as far as possible) in all the foregoing details, so as to make them prompt in action and less liable to error in case of emergency.

For further instruction or information please address the nearest office of the Company.

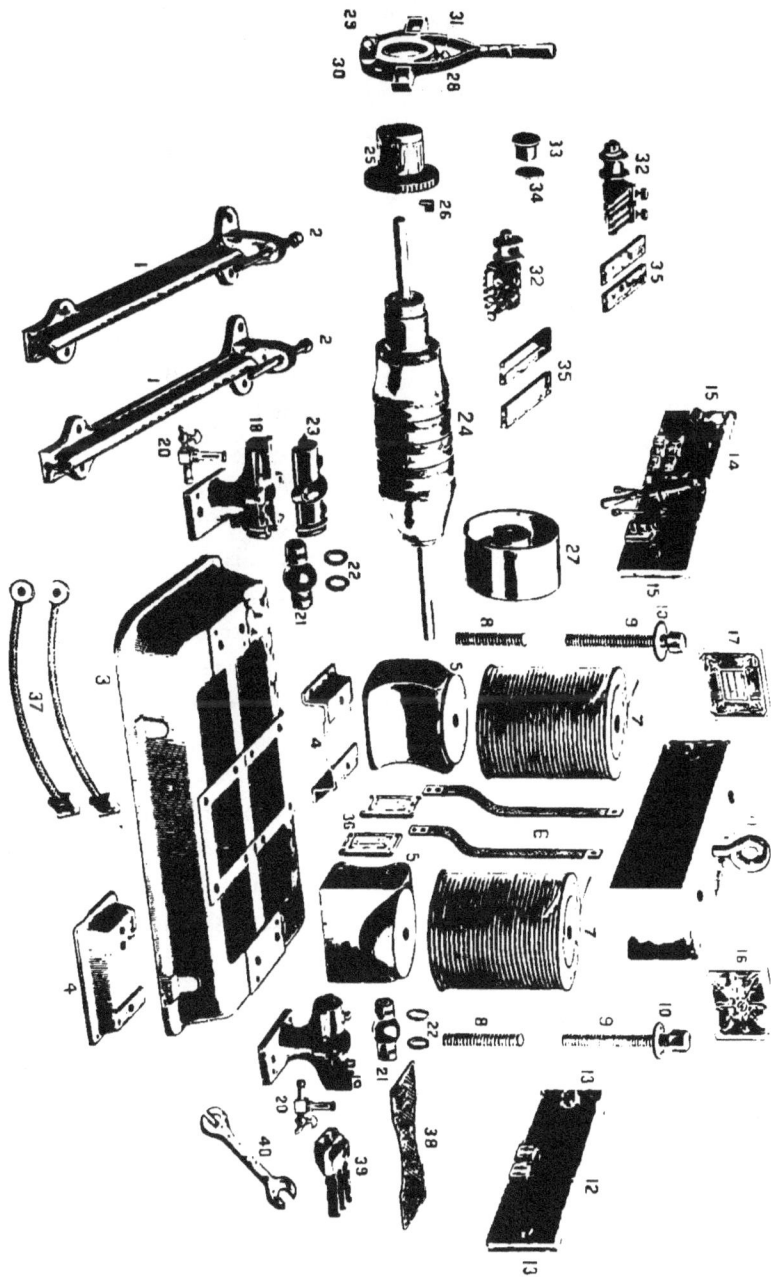

LIST OF PARTS, EDISON GENERATOR,
"1885 TYPE."

1. Rails.
2. Adjusting Rail-Bolts.
3. Bed-Plate.
4. Zinc Bases for Fields.
5. Pole Pieces.
6. Conductor Rods.
7. Field Coils and Cores.
8. Lower Screws. field cores to pole pieces.
9. Bolts for attaching keeper to pole pieces.
10. Washer for same.
11. Keeper.
12. Blackboard and field coil terminal blocks.
13. Bolts for same.
14. Head-board.
15. Bolts for same.
16. Rib Side-Plate.
17. Panel Side-Plate for Name-plate.
18. Pillow Block Case. Commutator End.
19. Pillow Block Complete. Pulley End.
20. Drip Cock for self-oiling bearings.

21. Bearing Sleeve for self-oiling bearings.
22. Rings for self-oiling bearings.
23. Cap for Pillow Block. Commutator End.
24. Armature complete.
25. Commutator complete.
26. Comt. Cap for ends of Armature coils.
27. Armature Pulley.
28. Brush Yoke.
29. Bolt for same.
30. Spring Washer for adjusting tension.
31. Thumb Screw for Yoke.
32. Brush-Holder Complete.
33. Insulating Blocks for Brush-Holder.
34. Insulating Washer for Brush-Holder.
35. Brushes.
36. Foot-Boards.
37. Brush-Holder Cables.
38. Wire Screen for protecting Armature.
39. Brush Filing Jig.
40. Generator Wrench.

CONNECTIONS FOR
.5, .75 AND 1.5 K.W. GENERATORS
KEEPER REGULATION.

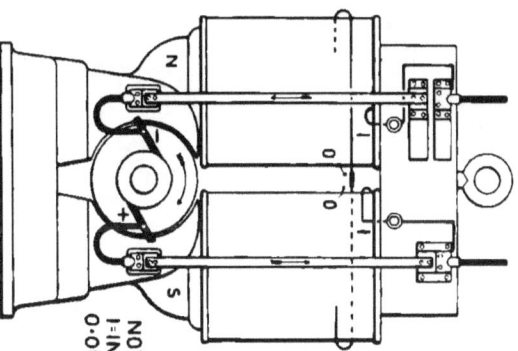

NOTE:
I=INSIDE END.
O-OUTSIDE.

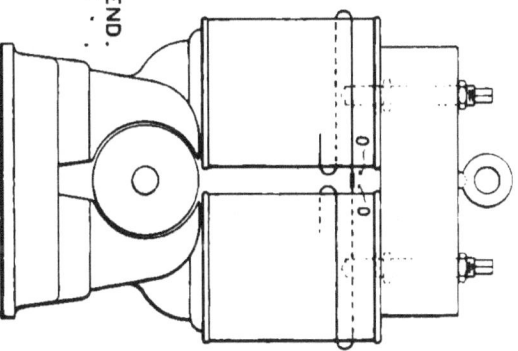

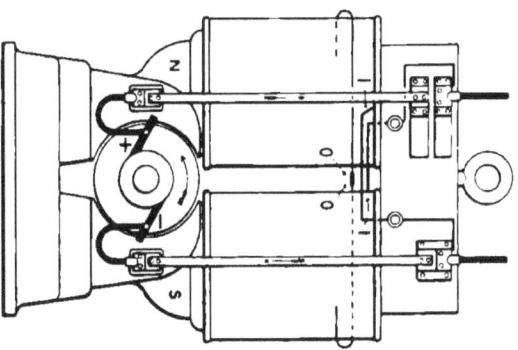

No.13055.

GENERAL ELECTRIC CO.

APR.28.'93.

CONNECTIONS FOR
EDISON BI-POLAR GENERATORS
SHUNT WOUND. 125 VOLTS.

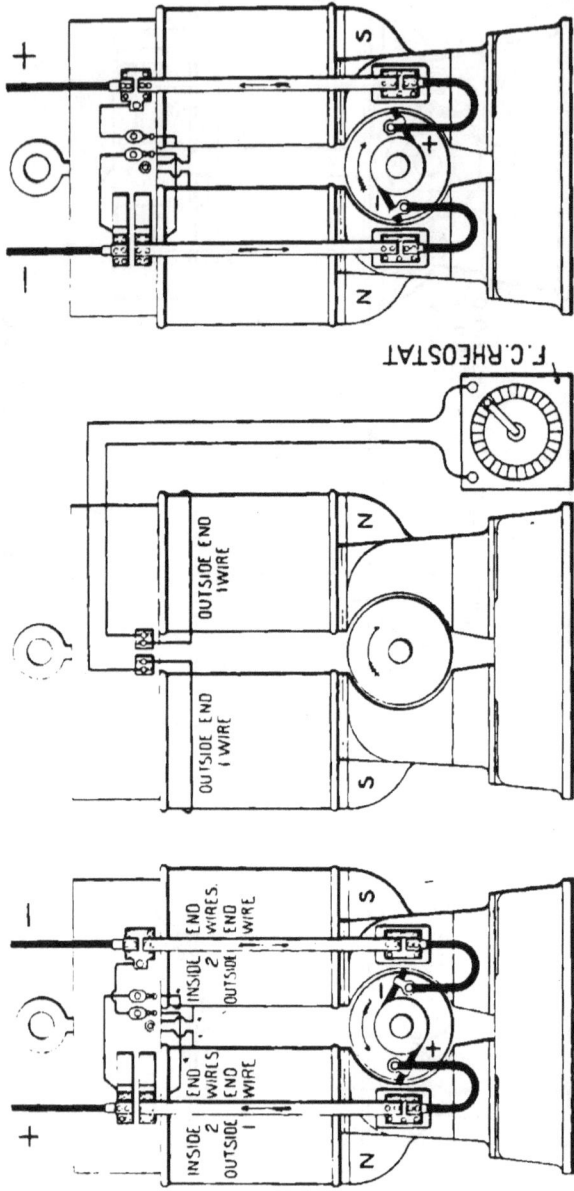

+

−

+

S

+

N

F.C.RHEOSTAT

N

OUTSIDE END 1 WIRE

OUTSIDE END 1 WIRE

S

−

+

INSIDE END WIRES. 2 OUTSIDE END 1 WIRE

INSIDE END WIRES 2 OUTSIDE END 1 WIRE

S

N

No.13004.   GENERAL ELECTRIC CO.   DEC 14.'92.

TYPE D AND SPHERICAL INCANDESCENT
GENERATORS.

The directions given in the preceeding pages will apply in large part to the installation and operation of the "D" and Spherical Incandescent Generators.

The accompanying diagrams and illustrations show the features of these machines which are not common to the Edison bipolar machines.

TYPE D GENERATORS
CLASSES 2 TO 15

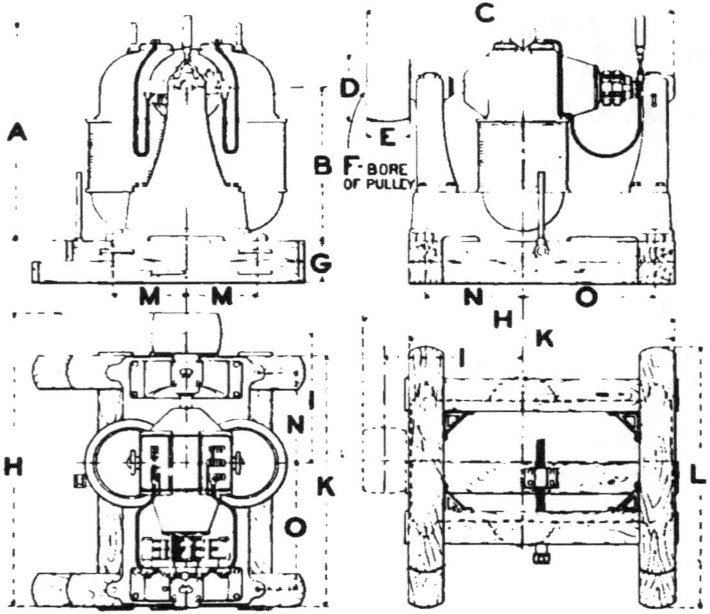
C
D
A
E
B
F - BORE OF PULLEY
G
M
M
N
H
O
K
I
N
H
K
O
I
L

CLASS	2	3	5	7½	10	15
NET WEIGHT*	340	530	720	1120	1490	2000
WEIGHT OF WOOD BED PLATE	45	45	50	60	90	110
KILOWATTS	2	3	5	7½	10	15
HORSE POWER TO DRIVE	3	4½	7½	11½	15	22½
SPEED	2500	2400	2000	1600	1600	1400
A	18 5/16	20 7/16	23 3/4	26 1/2	28 7/16	32 5/8
B ⌀	13 9/16	14	16 9/16	18 13/16	20 1/16	23 3/16
C	23 15/16	29 1/4	30 11/16	36 15/16	40 1/4	44 1/8
D ⌀	4	5	6	8	8	10
E	2	3	4	5	6	7
F ⌀	1	1 1/8	1 1/8	1 3/8	1 3/4	1 7/8
G	5 3/16	5 3/16	5 3/16	5 3/16	5 3/16	5 3/16
H	23 3/8	28 3/8	30 1/2	36 15/16	40 1/2	44 3/16
I	10 1/16	12 3/4	12 5/8	16 1/16	17 3/8	19 3/8
K	21 1/8	25	26 3/8	31 7/8	35	37 1/2
L	28 1/2	24 1/2	30	33 1/4	37	40 1/2
M	8 1/2	6 3/8	7 11/16	8 9/16	9	10 1/8
N	6 7/8	8 7/8	8 7/16	11 1/16	12 3/16	13 1/4
O	10 3/4	12 5/8	13 13/16	15 15/16	17 1/2	18 3/8

* WITHOUT BED PLATE App.: R. G. Reich

⌀ EXACT; ALL OTHER DIMENSIONS APPROXIMATE

No. 3618 General Electric Co. Jan. 2, 1893

TYPE D GENERATORS
CLASSES 20 TO 90

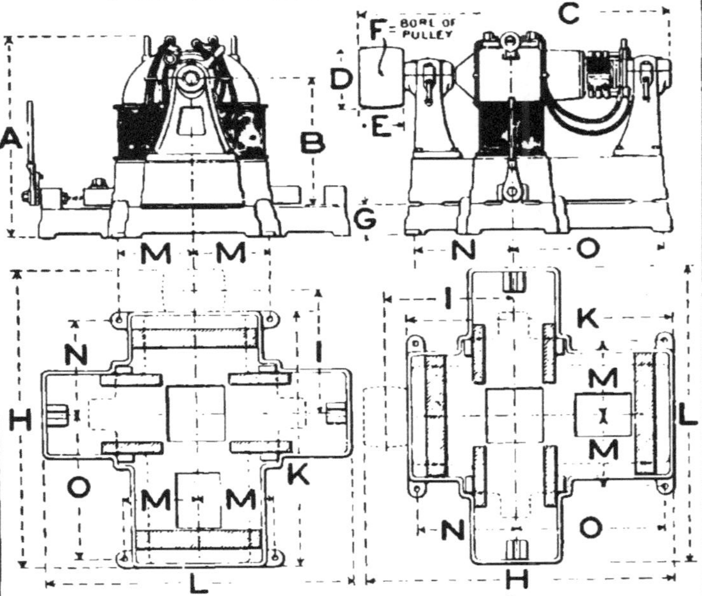
BORE OF PULLEY
A
B
C
D
E
F
G
H
I
K
L
M
N
O

No. 3617. General Electric Co Jan 2,'93

CLASS	20	25	30	40	50	62	90
NET WEIGHT*	3100	3675	4825	6325	7300	10325	15775
WEIGHT OF IRON BED PLATE	690	900	1050	1850	2150	2220	2720
KILOWATTS	20	25	30	40	50	62	90
HORSE POWER TO DRIVE	30	38	45	60	75	93	135
SPEED	1300	1225	1170	1125	1020	900	750
A	36 5/8	36 5/8	39 1/2	43 3/8	46 3/8	53 1/2	58 7/8
B ⊙	26 5/8	25 3/4	29 1/4	32 3/8	34 1/4	39 3/8	43 3/8
C	58 5/8	62 3/8	66 1/4	75 5/8	81 5/8	90 1/8	105 3/4
D ⊙	13 1/2	14	14 1/2	15 1/2	17	19	23
E	9	9	10	11	12	13	14
F ⊙	2	2 3/16	2 7/16	2 3/4	2 15/16	3 7/16	3 13/16
G	5 1/4	6	6 1/2	7 1/2	7 1/2	9 3/8	9 1/8
H	60 7/16	63 3/16	67	75 5/8	81 7/8	91 1/8	109 1/4
I	25 13/16	26 3/4	27 5/8	31 9/16	34 11/16	38 11/16	44 1/2
K	50 11/16	54	57 1/2	66 1/16	69 5/8	77	96
L	49 13/16	61 1/4	67 1/4	76 3/16	77 13/16	88 5/8	93
M	15 1/4	15 5/16	16 5/16	18 5/8	19 1/2	20 5/16	23 7/8
N	19	20 3/4	20 7/8	24 7/8	25 1/2	28 1/2	33 1/2
O	28 1/2	30 3/4	32 5/8	36 5/8	38 3/4	43	53 1/2

*Without bed plate. App. H.S. Reist

⊙ Exact; all other dimensions approximate.

CONNECTIONS OF D-2, D-3, D-5, D-7½, D-10, D-15
SHUNT GENERATORS.

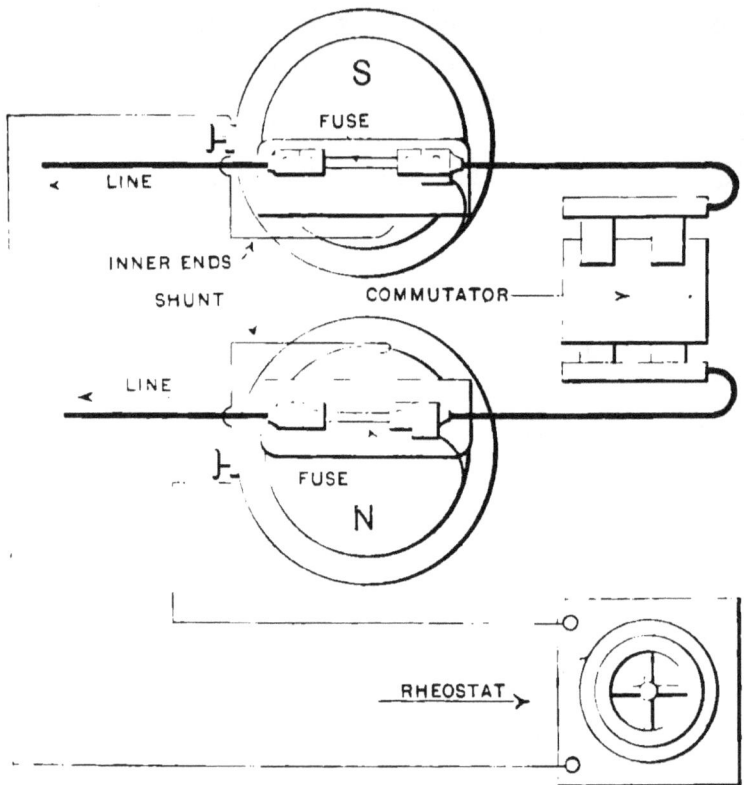

S

FUSE

LINE

INNER ENDS

SHUNT   COMMUTATOR

LINE

FUSE

N

RHEOSTAT

GENERAL ELECTRIC CO.

No. 3497.   March 31, 1892.

CONNECTIONS OF D-3, D-5, D-7½, D-10, D-15
125 VOLT COMPOUND GENERATORS.

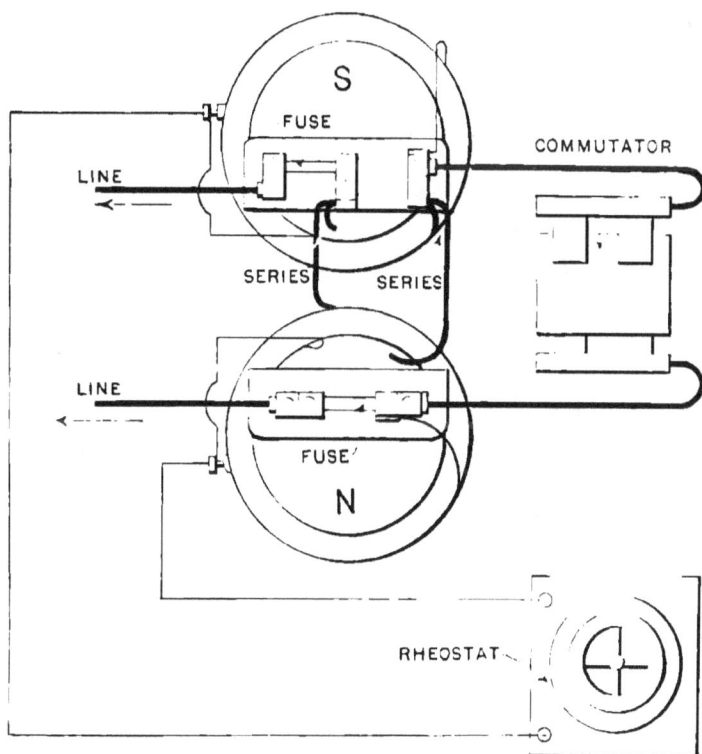

GENERAL ELECTRIC CO.

No. 3502.   April 8, 1892.

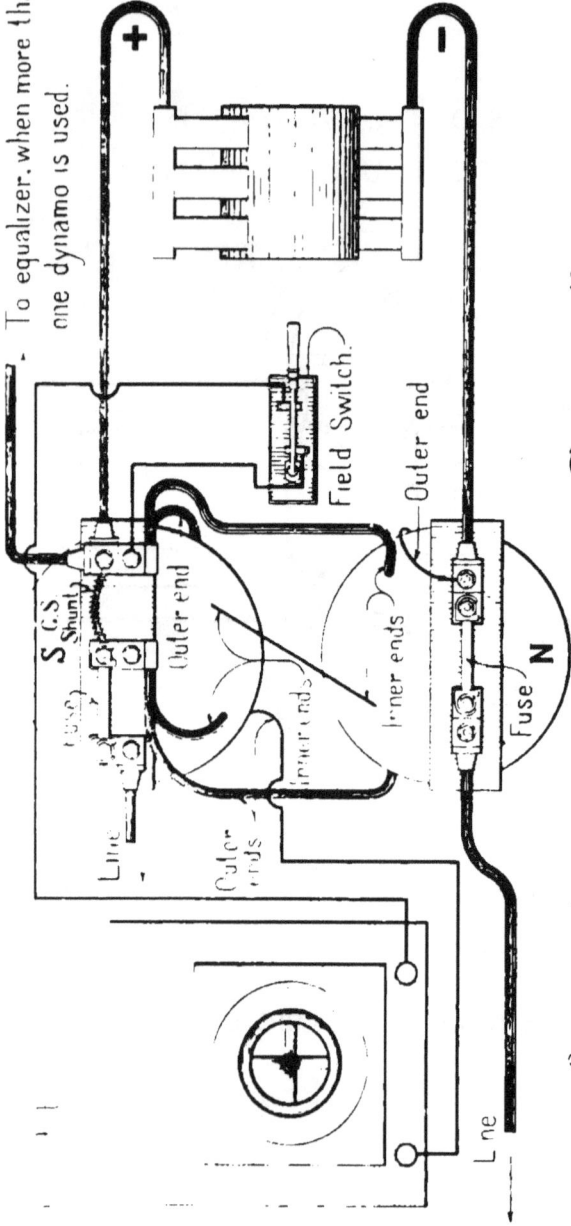

Connections of D-20,D-25,D-30,D-40,D-50,D-62,D-90. 125-Volt Generators.

To equalizer, when more than one dynamo is used.

Field Switch.

Outer end

Outer end

Inner ends

Inner ends

Outer ends

Fuse

N

S.C.S (Shunt)

Outer end

Line

Line

Nº 3455

COMMUTATOR DATA TYPE D GENERATORS.

GENERATOR.		Number of Segments.	Diameter of Active Surface.		Useful Length of Commutator.
Class.	Volts.		Normal.	Minimum.*	
2	125	32	2 15/16"	1 13/16"	1 11/16
2	250	64	3 3/8	2 1/8"	1 11/16"
2	500	64	3 3/8"	2 1/8"	1 11/16"
3	125		3 3/8	2 1/8"	1 11/16
3	250	64	3 3/8	2 1/8	1 11/16"
3	500	64	3 3/8	2 1/8"	1 11/16"
5	125	64	3 3/8"	2 1/8	3 3/16"
5	250	64	3 3/8	2 1/8	3 3/16"
5	500	64	3 3/8	2 1/8	3 3/16
7½	125	48	3"	1 7/8"	3 3/16
7½	250	64	3 3/8	2 1/8	3 3/16
7½	500	64	3 1/8"	2 1/8"	3 3/16
10	125	44	4 7/8	3 1/8"	4
10	250	56	4 7/8	3	4
10	500	64	4 7/8	3 1/8	4
15	125	44	4 7/8	3 1/2"	4
15	250	88	4 7/8	3 1/2	4
15	500	88	4 7/8	3 1/2	4
20	125	80	6	4 1/8"	
20	250	80	6	4 1/8	
20	500	80	6	4 1/8	
25	125	72	6 1/2"	4 7/8"	6 5/16
25	250	72	6 1/2	4 7/8	6 5/16
25	500	72	6 1/2	4 7/8	6 5/16
30	125	70 long	7	5 1/8	6 5/16
30	250	70 long	7	5 1/8	6 5/16"
30	500	70 short	7	5 1/8	5 1/16
40	125	60	7 7/8"	5 7/8"	6 3/8"
40	250	60	7 7/8	5 3/4	6 3/8
40	500	60	7 7/8"	5 7/8	6 3/8
50	125	50 long	8 1/4	6 1/4"	7 7/16"
50	250	50 long	8 1/4	6 1/4	7 7/16
50	500	50 short	8 1/4	6 1/4	5 1/16"
62	125	42	8 3/8"	6 1/4	7 1/2"
62	250	90 long	8 3/8	6 3/8	7 1/2
62	500	90 short	8 3/8"	6 3/8"	5 1/16"
90	125	44	10 3/8"	7 1/2	11 1/8
90	250	88	12 1/2"	10 7/8"	
90	500	88	12 1/2"	10 7/8"	

* Least possible safe thickness.

SPEEDS OF TYPE D GENERATORS.

KILOWATTS RATING AT 110, 220 AND 500 VOLTS.

2	3	5	7.5	10	15	20	25	30	40	50	62	80

AMPERES OF 100-130 VOLT GENERATORS.

18	27	45	68	91	136	182	227	272	364	454	566	818
	1920	1850	1650	1490	1300	1100	1050	1000	950	800	730	650
	2030	1910	1730	1470	1350	1150	1100	1050	1000	800	730	680
	2110	2000	1800	1540	1380	1250	1150	1100	1000	950	830	730
	2210	2080	1880	1600	1350	1350	1350	1150	1100	950	840	780
	2300	2150	1940	1680	1400	1900	1250	1900	1125	900	870	780
	2400	2240	2020	1730	1450	1350	1360	1250	1170	1050	900	810
	2500	2340	2130	1850	1500	1400	1350	1300	1290	1040	930	880

AMPERES OF 230-270 VOLT GENERATORS.

9	13.5	22.5	34	45	68	91	114	136	162	227	272	400
	2110	2000	1800	1540	1380	1300	1170	1100	1050	950	850	730
	2210	2700	1940	1680	1400	1250	1200	1150	1140	950	890	750
	2300	2150	1930	1680	1400	1600	1200	1900	1125	900	870	740
	2400	2340	2040	1700	1450	1850	1300	1250	1170	1030	900	810
	2500	2740	2130	1850	1400	1400	1350	1300	1290	1000	940	880

AMPERES OF 460-540 VOLT GENERATORS.

4	6	10	15	20	30	40	50	60	80	100	125	180
	2400	2540	2000	1730	1400	1700	1300	1250	1170	1050	950	840
	2750	2700	2150	1840	1350	1410	1300	1210	1300	1070	940	880
	940	2670	2540	1920	1600	1440	1400	1370	1200	1150	960	900

No 3395. Oct. 13, 1891.

Incandescent Dynamos.

Spherical Type - For Isolated Lighting.

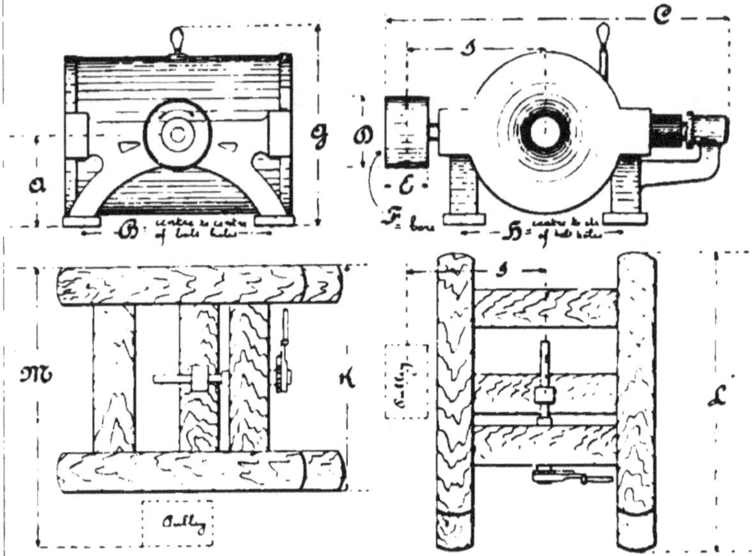

Class.	B I.	C I.	E I.	H I.
Net Weight.	700.	1200.	2250.	4400.
Speed.	1600.	1550	1250.	1150.
Lights - 16 C.P.	60.	125	250.	450.
Watts	4000	8000	16000.	30000.
A	8 3/4	9 1/2	12 7/8	15 3/4
B	19 3/4	25 1/2	32 1/2	40 1/2
C.	31	37 1/2	48	62 1/4
D	7	9	12	15
E.	5	7	10	12
F	1 1/2	1 7/8	2 3/8	2 7/8
G	—	27 1/2	33 3/4	38 1/2
H	14 1/2	17 1/2	23 1/2	28 3/4
I.	12 1/2	14	19 5/8	25 3/4
K.	17 1/2	21 3/8	27 3/8	33 1/2
L	30 3/4	38 1/2	45 1/2	54
M.	23 3/4	28 1/16	38 5/16	45 1/2

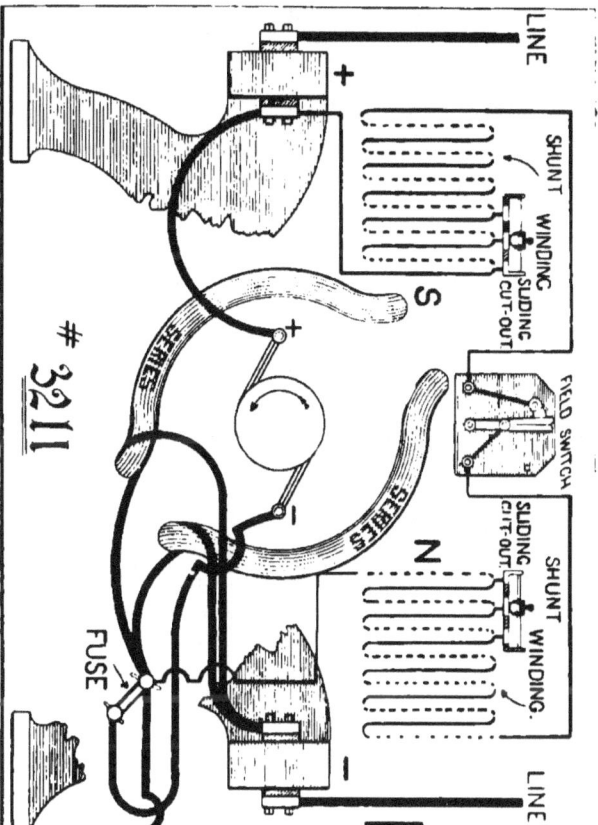

LINE

+

SHUNT WINDING

SLIDING CUT-OUT

S

FIELD SWITCH

SLIDING CUT-OUT

SHUNT WINDING.

N

SERIES

SERIES

+

I

I

3211

FUSE

—

LINE

CONNECTIONS
OF
SPHERICAL
INCANDESCENT
DYNAMOS.

June, 90.

App. G.C.R.

TO EQUALIZING
CONNECTION. WHERE MORE
THAN ONE DYNAMO IS USED

COMMUTATOR DATA SPHERICAL INCANDESCENT.

CLASS.	VOLTS.	K.W.	NUMBER SEGMENTS.	DIA. ACTIVE SURFACE.		USEFUL LENGTH OF COMMUTATOR.
				Normal.	*Minimum.	
B1	75	3.84	48	3 "	1½'	3¼"
B1	110		48	3 "	1½"	3¼"
C1	75	7.68	48	3 "	1½"	3¼¼"
C1	110	7.68	48	3	1½"	3¼¼'
E1	75	14.40	64	4½'	3¼'	4¼¼"
E1	110	14.40	88	4⅜"	3¼	4¼¼"
H1	75	28.80	44	7⅜	4½'	6⅝"
H1	110	28.80	64	5¼'	4½"	6⅞'

* Minimum is least safe diameter.

www.ingramcontent.com/pod-product-compliance
Lightning Source LLC
Chambersburg PA
CBHW022150090426
42742CB00010B/1451